Original title:
The Wonder in Christmas Moments

Copyright © 2024 Creative Arts Management OÜ
All rights reserved.

Author: Aurora Sinclair
ISBN HARDBACK: 978-9916-94-028-0
ISBN PAPERBACK: 978-9916-94-029-7

Starry Skies Over Frosty Fields

Snowflakes dance like little sprites,
While reindeer play in silly tights.
The stars above in gleeful cheer,
Whispering secrets for all to hear.

Puddles form where snowballs land,
Sliding contests go as planned.
Frosty breath in the cold night air,
Kids giggle in their frosty wear.

Mistletoe Dreams and Warmth

Beneath the mistletoe we stand,
With awkward grins, and clumsy plans.
A peck on cheeks, and laughter flows,
As awkwardness around us grows.

Grandpa's sweater, a vibrant hue,
Makes even the cat blurt out, "Boo!"
In every hug, there's warmth that's silly,
As we dance around, oh such a frilly!

Echoes of Laughter in the Air

Stockings hang with a curious twist,
And Dad forgets that he's on the list.
In every giggle, a new tale spins,
About Uncle Joe and the turkey wins.

Sisters fight for the biggest slice,
While Grandma hums, with hands so nice.
Chasing dogs under the mistletoe,
What a sight to see, a big furry show!

Cinnamon Scents and Candle Glow

Gingerbread men start to prance,
With licorice legs—they take a chance.
The candlelight flickers, shadows leap,
As pastry chefs try not to weep.

Sprinkles fly, the frosting's wild,
And in the corner, a giggling child.
Cookies crumble with a delightful sound,
As laughter and sweets abound.

Twilight Reflections of Togetherness

Snowflakes dance upon our heads,
Laughter echoes, as mischief spreads.
Uncle Joe trips, the turkey flies,
Feathers scattered, oh my, what a prize!

Grandma's cookies, slightly burnt,
Yet we cheer, not a little hurt.
A game of charades, all in jest,
Guessing wild, we're truly blessed!

Glimpses of Joy in the Ordinary

Socks mismatched, the kids all cheer,
'They're fashionable!' they declare with glee.
Hot cocoa spills on the pillow fights,
Merry madness on festive nights.

Two left feet on the dance floor bob,
Grandpa winks, giving it a job.
Nutcracker soldiers start to break,
Oh dear, what a holiday shake!

From Distant Lands We Gather

Auntie flies in from afar,
Bringing tales of a bizarre spar.
A goat wore her hat on a train,
We all howl, oh what a gain!

From places wide, we come as one,
Sipping punch, oh what fun!
Gifts wrapped up in duct tape bright,
Open slowly, what a sight!

Melodies of Shared Destiny

Carols sung with a funny twist,
Uncle Bob's turn brings the mist.
Off-key notes fill up the air,
Laughter escapes; we haven't a care.

Eggnog spills on the family tree,
Uncle Ted chuckles, 'That's just me!'
Together we laugh, dance, and sway,
Creating memories, come what may!

Joy Wrapped in Tinsel Trails

Tinsel tangled in my hair,
A kitty stole my festive flair.
Cookies burned, just like my dreams,
Yet laughter bursts at family seams.

Snowflakes dance like holiday spright,
My dad just slipped, what a funny sight!
The lights are blinkin', oh so bright,
We trip and laugh, what pure delight!

The Spirit of Giving

Wrapped gifts hidden, oh what fun,
A prankster's job has just begun!
I left a note, 'Please open me',
Then hid in case the cat should see.

Grandma's sweater, two sizes wide,
It fits the dog; we laugh and hide.
A red-nosed reindeer? Quite absurd,
With a jingle bell meow that's heard!

Cherished Memories Beneath the Tree

Under the tree, we find some loot,
A sock with rocks? A seasoned brute!
We giggle hard, the presents sway,
A cat's in there, oh what a play!

Mom's baking pies, they're not her best,
I thank my stars; I'll take the rest!
The laughter echoes, isn't it grand?
With silly tales, hand in hand.

Firelit Huddles and Holiday Tales

Around the fire, we tell tall tales,
Of slippery slopes and failed holiday fails.
Dad's dramatic flair, so wild and free,
Sparks fly as we laugh, oh silly me!

The marshmallows toast, but not too neat,
My sister's pout, a sugar-filled treat.
We roast ridiculous stories, quite a show,
In firelit huddles, we glow and glow!

Beauty in Moments of Stillness

Snow falls softly on the lane,
Cats in coats, they think they're sane.
A frosty nose, a friendly laugh,
Hot cocoa spills—now that's our craft.

We check our lists, we make them twice,
Santa's sleigh is full of mice!
With twinkling lights that birth a cheer,
We dance and trip, then shed a tear.

Embracing the Spirit of Generosity

Gifts piled high, oh what a sight,
Grandma's fruitcake—what a fright!
We share the load and take our share,
But whose is this? I think it's hair!

Cookies vanish, crumbs abound,
Potluck chaos swirling 'round.
A dance-off breaks in the living room,
A warm embrace? Or just the gloom?

Delicious Bites of Happiness

Candy canes and jelly beans,
A food fight breaks, amidst the greens!
Chili burns, let's call a truce,
And hide the snacks, there goes the moose!

Grandpa's pie is quite the scene,
Olive salad, not so keen.
Still, we feast and share a laugh,
As Aunt Betty sings from the bath!

Mirth in the Glow of Lights

Lights twinkle bright upon the tree,
Uncle Joe's dressed like a bee!
The ornaments drop, it's quite the show,
The cat's in the tree, oh no, oh no!

We gather 'round with hearts so free,
Singing off-key, just let it be.
As laughter bursts like popcorn pops,
We make a memory, and then it stops.

The Symphony of Homemade Wishes

Whisking eggs, flour flies wide,
Grandma's nose is a culinary guide.
The dog swipes the cookie we planned,
Now it's a battle we hadn't planned.

Kids in the kitchen, laughter ignites,
Frosting fights turn into sweet bites.
Uncle Joe sneezes, the cake's in distress,
Mom's wearing icing—a glittery mess!

The Warmth of a Shared Blanket

Two cats sprawled on a one-seat chair,
Purring tunes fill the cozy air.
Bobby's feet—cold as ice—
Stealing warmth, they're not very nice.

Siblings curl like warm pretzels here,
Hot cocoa spills—oh dear, oh dear!
Tickle wars break the truce unwritten,
Mom yells, 'Stop! Who's been smitten?'

Glorious Moments by Firelight

Marshmallows roast on the popsicle sticks,
Charlie's face lights with sweet little tricks.
The fire crackles, a s'mores design,
Who knew laughter could taste so divine?

Granny false-snorts on the last joke told,
The warmth of the moment, too precious to mold.
Fingers sticky and well-fed smiles beam,
This is the magic that comes from the cream!

Enchanted Walks in the Snow

Sidewalks sparkle with powdery bliss,
Snowball fights, don't fall for the kiss!
Sledding down hills that look like cake,
Who knew winter could be such a break?

Three coats on, yet one's still cold,
"Who's the genius?" Grandma scolded bold.
Laughing, we trudge through the snowshoes' maze,
Each step a dance, a silly ballet.

The Gift of Togetherness

In sweaters matching, we do clatter,
As Uncle Joe spills gravy - what a splatter!
Grandma's cookies stack so high,
We laugh till we hiccup, oh my oh my!

The one-eyed tree topper, we try to fix,
While siblings bicker over silly tricks.
Cards all misplayed, but we'll play on,
In this jolly chaos, we find our dawn.

Chimney Smoke and Warm Embraces

The smoke curls up and fills the room,
As Dad's old jokes bring endless gloom.
Hot cocoa spills on Grandma's rug,
But oh, that mug, it's a cozy hug!

The cat's in the tree, a sight so grand,
With tinsel wrapped snugly, it just can't stand.
We'll rescue our biscuits from a hungry pup,
In this fest of chaos, we just won't stop!

Time Slows in a Flurry

As snowflakes swirl, we dance and twirl,
Hot pies in the oven start to unfurl.
With every tick of the clock, we laugh,
'Till Dad tries to tell his old photograph!

The lights outside flash like a grand parade,
While kids chase each other, oh what a charade!
We'll trip over toys, but we'll hold on tight,
In moments so silly, we rise with delight!

Stars that Guide Our Hearts

Sipping cider under twinkling skies,
Where Grandma's jokes bring tears to our eyes.
The star on the tree winks with a flair,
While we bicker about who gets the chair!

As we share our dreams with giggles and grins,
And recount our tales of past little sins.
With every goofy grin, our hearts take flight,
In this festival of joy, all feels so right!

A Time for Togetherness

The turkey's run away, oh what a sight,
In the kitchen, chaos takes the flight.
Mom's looking frantic, dad's lost his shoe,
The dog's got the ham, he's in on the crew!

Family laughter fills the air,
Uncle Fred's jokes, we all must bear.
Counting the gifts, we lose track of time,
But who needs precision when chaos is prime?

Elves at Play in Twinkling Light

In the workshop, elves are buzzing around,
Spinning toys and falling to the ground.
With ladders wobbling, they take a wild leap,
Who knew gift-making could lead to a heap?

Tinsel tangled in their hats and hair,
Jingle bells ringing, with quite the flair.
One elf's gone missing, oh what a fright,
Found hiding in cookies, munching all night!

Joy's Sweet Symphony

Carols are sung, off-key and loud,
Audience members, quite a bit cowed.
A cat on the piano, it's pure serenade,
With jingles and meows, the pets invade!

Grandma's on stage, she's lost her attire,
Wearing a scarf when she meant to retire.
But smiles spread wide, as laughter erupts,
In this silly fiasco, joy erupts!

Paths of Pine and Peace

A stroll through the woods, the snow's a delight,
But I slip on ice, oh what a plight!
A snowman waves, but he's lost his hat,
While squirrels throw snowballs, imagine that!

Pine needles stick to my cozy scarf,
While the children giggle, they know how to snarf.
In this frosty maze, we all feel so free,
Even if falling's our new specialty!

Dreams Captured in Ornaments

Hanging baubles on a tree,
Fell off, now they're laughing at me.
Lights are tangled, a cat's on the prowl,
Singing loudly, a squirrel's foul growl.

Cookies baked without a plan,
Burnt edges dance, the dough did a jam.
Santa's list got lost in the fray,
Now he's gifting socks that smell all day.

Wrapping paper stuck on my shoe,
Presents shuffled, oh what a view.
Dancing elves in my living room,
Swept away by the cookie perfume.

Giggles echo, a snowball fight,
Turns to chaos, what a delight!
Dreams captured in these silly, sweet times,
Laughter ringing, like jingle bell chimes.

The Tenderness of Old Carols

Singing loudly 'round the fire,
Uncle Joe's off-key, but we admire.
Grandma's knitting, a snowman's head,
While Dad drops lyrics, here comes the dread.

Merry voices from the past,
Hot cocoa spills, oh what a blast.
Carols turn to giggles and cheers,
As we debate the best holiday beers.

Now 'Jingle Bells' becomes a song,
Of people slipping, where they belong.
Everything's funny, from now till dawn,
As we sing our hearts out, and keep the fun on.

Nostalgia drifts like the scent of pine,
Every note, a laugh, oh so fine.
Old carols painted with smiles galore,
Reminding us of laughter, and always wanting more.

Facets of Joy in Every Gesture

Wrapped in lights, a holiday race,
Did you see Mom's confused face?
Gifts wrapped in paper, too small, too big,
Uncle Fred gives a hug, does a jig.

Decorating cookies, a flour fight,
Snowflakes falling, a playful sight.
Every smile a sparkle, a twinkle so bright,
As we munch on delights into the night.

Laughter echoes, a gag gift found,
Tangled in ribbons, we spin around.
Joy purveyors of silly antics,
Facets of laughter, like magic manics.

From silly hats to odd jingle toys,
Each moment we share, endless joys.
In every gesture there's a spark we treasure,
A banquet of silliness, beyond all measure.

Frosty Windows and Cozy Stories

Frosty windows hide giggles, oh dear,
Stories unfold as we stick close and cheer.
Hot cocoa spills, laughter's delight,
Tell us again about Santa's flight.

Blankets piled high, a fort we create,
The cat pounces in, claiming his fate.
Whispers of mischief, secrets to share,
As we poke fun at Dad's silly hair.

Outside, the snowflakes begin their dance,
In here, the warmth gives us the chance.
Every chuckle and smile fills the space,
Frosty panes conceal our happy embrace.

Nostalgic stories, a cozy retreat,
Turn the mundane into a holiday feat.
Amidst the laughter, a memory so pure,
With every moment, our hearts find a cure.

Stories Wrapped in Tinsel

A cat caught in the twinkle lights,
Chasing shadows on frosty nights.
Grandma's yelling, 'Not the tree!'
As Uncle Bill spills the punch with glee.

Little ones in matching sweaters,
Swapping toys like it's a treasure.
Each present looks a little lopsided,
With bows that are mysteriously misguided.

The reindeer snacks turn out to be,
Grandpa's leftover jerky, oh me!
Yet laughter fills the chilly air,
In every moment, joy is everywhere.

A Wish Upon a Pine

I found a squirrel in Santa's hat,
Who claimed he's had a chat with that rat.
With each wish upon the pine,
He'd wiggle his tail and say, 'It's fine!'

The ornaments are quite bizarre,
A pickle, a shoe, and a candy bar.
Mom insists that's how it's done,
While Dad's too busy just having fun.

Underneath those twinkling stars,
We debated if we should drive or ride in cars.
The laughter echoed through the night,
As we wrapped our dreams, all cozy and tight.

The Magic in Homemade Cookies

Flour fights and sneaky bites,
Of dough that vanished in the lights.
Mom's recipe, a mystery,
Is now just crumbs and history.

Sprinkles flew like confetti bright,
As we laughed 'til aching with delight.
The oven beeped, we cheered, hooray,
Then burned the batch in a goofy way!

With milk spills and frosting plans,
We built a cookie that kinda spans.
A crooked smile, one eye too wide,
But in our hearts, we took great pride.

Underneath the Garland

A toddler's giggle, a puppy's bark,
Underneath the garland, not too dark.
A treasure hunt for gifts galore,
But somehow found Mom's slippers, what a score!

Santa's sleigh stalled in the yard,
With stags playing cards, oh that's quite hard!
They say one's naughty, the other nice,
But both are here for Mom's famous spice.

In fuzzy socks we dance and prance,
Making silly faces in a playful trance.
As bells ring loud, the fun unfurls,
In every corner, laughter twirls.

Frosty Breath and Golden Laughter

Snowflakes dance like clumsy elves,
Children giggle, no one shelves.
Sleds fly down, a frosty race,
Hot cocoa spills, a chocolate chase.

Scarves wrapped tight, noses bright,
Snowmen wobble, what a sight!
A dog leaps, the snow goes flying,
In cold fun, there's no denying.

Gloves are lost, mittens paired,
Every trip ends with someone scared.
A snowball flies with a squishy sound,
Laughter echoes all around.

Bonfire crackles, marshmallows roast,
Stories shared that we love most.
Frosty breath and laughter blend,
Joy in chaos, on that we depend.

Heartstrings Tied in Red and Green

Lights twinkle like old friends,
Tangled cords, where does it end?
Grandma's dress, a vibrant flare,
We all wear our holiday care.

Bows that slip, and gifts that trip,
A wrapped cat gives us a flip!
Cheerful tunes from somewhere near,
Singing loud, we spread the cheer.

Cookies gone, crumbs in a trail,
Who knew sweets could be so frail?
A Christmas sweater, oh so bright,
With reindeer putting up a fight.

Heartstrings tied in colors bold,
Every laugh, a memory told.
In every mix-up, close we grow,
In this season, love will flow.

A Tapestry of Family and Friends

A table spread, the chairs too tight,
Uncle Joe's hat is quite a sight.
A joke goes bad, the laughter roars,
Grandma's pie? It's gone from floors!

Stories shared, secrets spilled,
Sibling rivalries, overfilled.
Who made the mess? It's hard to tell,
But laughter wraps us very well.

A game of charades leads to a fall,
A drunk turkey makes the call.
In every mishap, bonds we find,
A tapestry woven, heart entwined.

Family quirks, they steal the show,
Every moment, love will grow.
Together we shine, a dazzling blend,
In all the chaos, we're the best trend.

Glimmers of Joy in Everyday Rituals

Morning mugs of frothy cheer,
Spices blend, the scent so clear.
A sprinkle here, a dash of that,
Makin' cookies, it's a spat!

Wrapping gifts in a hasty dance,
Tape stuck in the wrong circumstance.
Tinsel fights with hairdos grand,
It's a battle, oh look at that hand!

Carols sung off-key with glee,
When karaoke's 'just for me'.
Holiday jokes make eyes roll,
But in this joy, we fill our souls.

Glimmers of joy in every deed,
In holiday cheer, we plant the seed.
With laughter ringing, let's embrace,
These joyful moments, our warmest space.

The Gift of Stillness

In a quiet room, we sit and stare,
Watching the cat debate a chair.
With half a ribbon, it wrestles tight,
While we sip cocoa—what a sight!

A tree adorned with mismatched flair,
Mom's cookies stuck to the kitchen air.
Dad spilled tinsel everywhere in a rush,
Now each step feels like a holiday crush.

Grandma's snores fill the peaceful night,
Counting sheep, or maybe a bite?
The dog dreams big, a bark in sleep,
What secrets does the winter keep?

Wrapped gifts with more tape than grace,
Can we fit this madness in one space?
With laughter echoing, we find delight,
In this stillness, everything feels right.

Frosty Breezes

Winds blow brisk, but so do hats,
Frosty whispers, and cheeky chats.
Snowflakes dance, oh what a sight,
A snowman waves, though not quite right!

Parks full of laughter, giggles and falls,
Sledding so fast, hear the calls!
With every tumble, the giggles rise,
We land in snow, oh what a surprise!

Hot cocoa treats mixed with marshmallows,
Mom's eggnog giggles, her favorite fellows.
So warm inside from winter fun,
We'll trade these stories, one by one.

Heartfelt Wishes

Cards piled high, with glitter and glue,
We hope for gifts, but wish for stew.
Big Uncle Joe sings off-key,
Yet his grin brings cheer, can't you see?

A wish for socks, but not too plain,
Who needs more knits after the last refrain?
A neighbor's cat bars the door,
With meow and purr, what a festive bore!

Greetings exchanged, some silly songs,
While we dance to jingles, how could we go wrong?
Heartfelt antics fuel our night,
In these gatherings, everything feels bright.

Glittering Ornaments and Kindred Spirits

Ornaments hung with tender mishaps,
Some lose their hooks, making us gasp.
Grandpa declares he's the best tree,
But his sneezes startle the family!

Twinkling lights flicker, one goes dead,
A scavenger hunt now for the thread.
A sticky finger takes a bite,
From last year's candy - oh, what a fright!

With stories shared round the old fire,
We laugh at slips, and mistakes we admire.
Together we find what warmth can bring,
In a room where love makes the heart sing!

Sledding Beneath a Moonlit Sky

The hill is ready, our sleds await,
With laughter boundless, we can't be late.
Under a moon, we take our flight,
Hollering joy as we slide in delight!

Fingers cold, cheeks ablaze,
In this frosty night, we dare to maze.
Hit a tree but bounce back free,
Nothing beats how fun this can be!

Each trip down, the giggles swell,
Sharing stories, oh do tell!
With stars above and friends beside,
We embrace the thrill of the snowy ride!

Magic Within the Snowflakes

Snowflakes twirl and dance down low,
Landing on my frosty nose,
I chase them down, oh what a show,
While neighbors stare as laughter flows.

Hot cocoa spills, my hands all cold,
I slip on ice, my pride will break,
But in this chill, a joy untold,
Each slip just adds to my mistake.

The dog is rolling, what a sight,
Snowballs flying, oh what a fight,
He thinks he's fierce, yet he's a pup,
In snowy chaos, we both erupt.

A snowman formed with a floppy hat,
He stands so proud but leans a bit,
I swear he blinked, could it be that?
In winter's game, we've lost the wit.

Whispers of the Yuletide

Santa's list must be misplaced,
He sent me socks instead of toys,
I shake my fist, 'tis such a waste,
While kiddos squeal with gleeful noise.

The cat's atop the Christmas tree,
Swatting stars as if to say,
'Get down from there, you fool, that's me!'
With every paw, he mocks the day.

Cookies vanish, crumbs in sight,
I thought I baked, but who can say?
Perhaps the elves stole them last night,
While dreams of sugarplum ballet.

The carolers sing, though out of tune,
They dance around the neighbor's yard,
With jingle bells under the moon,
Laughing at our holiday card.

Twinkling Lights and Silent Nights

Twinkling lights on the house next door,
Look like a runway for UFOs,
Wonder if they'll ask for more,
As I climb up to adjust my bows.

My string of lights just won't cooperate,
They blink, they flash, then they just die,
I shout, 'You'll be my Christmas fate!'
As I watch the neighbors pass by.

The dog runs through, a blur of fur,
Knocking ornaments right off the shelf,
His looks that say, 'I'm quite the cur!'
While I just laugh, "Oh, great, myself!"

In silent nights, we gather round,
With cocoa cups and tales to share,
Amidst the chaos, joy is found,
Amidst the laughs, we break the stare.

A Hearth's Embrace

The hearth is crackling, lights aglow,
Grandma's cookies, a favorite bite,
But flour fights—oh, what a show!
The kitchen chaos reflects the night.

A grand roast spoils, the timer's lies,
Smoke alarms sing their high-pitched song,
While dinner guests with hungry eyes,
Are left to wait, and wait too long.

Jingle bells ring, kids dance about,
Spilling juice on the carpet anew,
With laughter, screams, and joyful shout,
They're sure to leave a dubious clue.

In this warm nook, with love all around,
Every mishap brings us more cheer,
Remembered laughs forever abound,
In a place where holiday's dear.

Evergreen Hues of Hope

In the tree's embrace, I found a sock,
It's bigger than the present, what a shock!
The cat decided, it's her new throne,
Pine-scented laughter, in our home.

Ribbons tangled like a pasta dish,
Wrapping gifts? Oh, that's my wish!
Tape sticks to fingers, it's quite the game,
Who knew the holidays could be so tame?

Cookies left for Santa, chocolate delight,
But with my luck, they'll vanish tonight!
Nibble and giggle, crumbs everywhere,
Santa's got competition—my dog, beware!

Lights that twinkle in colors so bright,
But one string flickers, oh what a sight!
I dance like a fool, caught in a spell,
Electricity bringing, oh so much hell!

Wrapped in Wool and Wonder

Wrapped in wool, I look like a ball,
My grandma's knitting, it's a cozy install.
Mittens too fuzzy, I can't hold a drink,
Spilling hot cocoa, let me rethink!

Under the mistletoe, a chance for a kiss,
But my uncle appears, and that's amiss.
He aims for my cheek, I dodge and I flee,
Turns out I've skill, when it's family!

The snowman I built, a jolly old chap,
Stole my carrot, thank you very crap!
His nose now a twig, what a great fall,
He's still the best buddy, at least tall!

Sleigh bells are ringing, oh what a groove,
But I tripped on the rug, so let me move!
Rolling to laughter, with all of my might,
I'll be the star of this holiday night!

Chiming Bells and Cheerful Songs

Chiming bells ring, they call out my name,
But I stepped on the cat, and now I'm to blame.
Her meow is a symphony of pure chaos,
Christmas morning? More like a clinic of pathos!

Songs fill the air, off-key like a troll,
I sing with delight, but lost my control.
The dog joins in, howling out loud,
A holiday concert, to make us all proud!

Wrapping up presents, it's an art I declare,
Until paper's gone, and I've found a spare.
Mom's old calendar, I wrap with my flair,
"Do not open," I scribble, with utmost care!

Eggnog's a treasure, I raise up my cup,
But my cousin chugs all, what an abrupt!
Now we're all tipsy, sharing sweet cheer,
This Christmas morning will go down in sheer fear!

Holiday Hues in Frosted Frames

Frosted frames show a snowy small town,
But my nose is red, like a clown in a gown.
The snowballs thrown, they fly with a twist,
And ended on my sister's new pink wrist!

Lights on the roof, a festive galore,
But I climbed up high, then forgot how to soar.
Down I fell gently, not quite in control,
Snow turned to tumble, straight to my soul!

Gingerbread houses, we built with pure glee,
But ants moved in, they looked happy as three.
Now the candy's all gone, just crumbs in sight,
Next year we'll bake, out of sheer delight!

Caroling neighbors, with hats on their heads,
Singing off-key, like they're "are we dead?"
But laughter erupts, as we join in the song,
This holiday season, we all just belong!

Comfort Found in Simple Pleasures

Cookies crumble on the floor,
A dog sneaks in, wants more.
Laughter echoes through the house,
As we hide sweets from the mouse.

Lights flicker, a dance of glee,
Unmatched tinsel on the tree.
Grandma's sweater, bright and loud,
Worn with pride, we all applaud.

Silent nights filled with cheer,
Hiding gifts from prying dear.
Pine smells mix with baked delight,
Yawning pets join in the fight.

Snowflakes fall, dive and swirl,
Kids chase dreams, give it a whirl.
Hot cocoa spills, oh what a mess,
But in chaos, we find our bliss.

Radiating Joy Through Traditions

Singing carols out of tune,
Caught the cat; oh, what a swoon!
Dad's attempts at festive flair,
Mismatched socks and wild hair.

Hats and scarves piled too high,
Family photos make us cry.
Grandma says it's all her fault,
When we trip and nearly halt.

Secret Santa's big reveal,
Pranks and giggles, lots to steal.
Wrapping paper takes the floor,
Chaos reigns—a holiday chore.

Dinner's served—a table spread,
We all laugh, but what was said?
Ugly sweaters, munchies near,
In each moment, joy is clear.

Ephemeral Beauty of the Season

Snowmen wobble, take a fall,
Carrot noses roll, that's all.
Two lumps of coal became a stare,
While kids giggle in the air.

Stars twinkle with a wink,
Flavored popcorn makes us think.
Holiday lights, a blinking spree,
Chasing shadows, let us be.

Whispers float in winter's chill,
Eggnog spills, a funny thrill.
Cousins poke their heads around,
Sharing jokes that soon astound.

Mom's fruitcake—oh, what a gift,
Takes a dive, no chance to lift.
But in the mess, we dance and spin,
Finding joy in where we've been.

Wrapped in the Spirit of Thanks

Grateful hearts and cheerful plates,
Family feasts for all our mates.
Spilling beans, oh what a tale,
Misplaced jabs, but we won't fail.

Thankful for the turkey's fate,
A dance-off makes us celebrate.
Funny hats and goofy grins,
In these moments, joy begins.

Pine cone crafts, we make a fuss,
Nature's gifts—let's ride the bus!
Uncle Jim's a clown today,
Cracking jokes in a silly way.

Toasting mugs with steaming brew,
All our love wrapped up anew.
In this chaos, laughter sings,
With every heart, a joy it brings.

Laughter Wrapped in Fabric

Socks that don't match come out to play,
Grandma's knitting gone slightly astray.
A scarf that's three sizes too big, oh dear,
Yet we laugh as we wrap it around, never fear!

Chasing the cat in the holiday light,
Draped in tinsel, what a silly sight!
We giggle and dash, those ornaments fly,
While Santa's list whispers, 'Don't ask why.'

Wearing a sweater like a fashion faux pas,
With reindeer that dance, and a big shiny star.
Each laugh rings out as we trim up the tree,
In this joyful chaos, we're merry and free!

Cinnamon rolls baking, the aroma so sweet,
Yet someone forgot to set the timer's beat.
With smoke and a giggle, we fix our mistake,
Laughter's the frosting on every cake!

Nostalgic Hues of the Season

Remember the carolers out in the snow,
They sang off-key but we loved the show.
With mittens too tight, we fumbled our treats,
And laughed at the snowball fight in the streets!

The lights on the house, oh what a bright mess,
One blue bulb flashing, the rest in distress.
We danced round the tree, in our jammies so snug,
While tripping on tinsel, we gave Santa a hug!

Mom's special fruitcake, a mystery delight,
With ingredients hidden, it gave quite a fright.
Yet we all took a slice, just to be kind,
Laughing as we vowed never again to find!

Each year it's the same, with joy and a cheer,
We raise our mugs high, to friends far and near.
Nostalgia nothing, just silly old glee,
With smiles wrapped tightly as gifts 'neath the tree!

The Enchantment of Shared Stories

Gather 'round the fire, let stories ignite,
Of the time Uncle Joe got lost in plain sight.
When Grandma went searching for cookies to bake,
And found only socks that she hoped wouldn't take!

We recall the mishaps of holidays past,
From hanging lights high to a turkey cast.
Each tale grows taller, with laughter we weave,
As we clutch at our sides, with hearts on our sleeves!

With cookies all crumbled and punch spilled on floor,
We share all our blunders, there's always room for more.
Each laugh is a thread, each chuckle a gift,
In this patchwork of moments, our spirits do lift!

So here's to the tales that bring us together,
In sparkly pajamas, or whatever the weather.
May we share every story, with joy that abounds,
In laughter we find all our hearts' merry sounds!

A Hearth that Warms the Soul

The logs in the fire crackle and pop,
As Aunt Edna's stories just never will stop.
Her cookies are legendary, chewy and bright,
But on the last batch, she forgot the sweets' light!

With hot cocoa in hand, we're cozy and stuffed,
But Timmy just found the marshmallows too rough.
He sneezes then giggles, his face all aglow,
As we scatter the fluff like fresh snow below!

While dad tells his jokes, the punchline's a twist,
A laugh shared is magic, a moment we missed.
In our mismatched pajamas, we snuggle and cheer,
For all the small moments we hold oh so dear!

Under twinkling lights, our laughter's the spark,
In the warmth of this place, not a soul stands in dark.
As we share in this joy, no chill meets the heart,
Together at the hearth, we'll never depart!

Traces of Joy in Each Corner

Cookies left out, crumbs on the floor,
A snack for the jolly, oh what a score!
Santa's belly, round and so wide,
Is it him or the cookies that's taken a ride?

Tinsel on llamas, a sight to behold,
Singing carols while sipping hot gold.
Mittens mismatched, but oh what a style,
Wrapped in laughter, we'll go the extra mile.

Pine needles dropping, our tree's in a funk,
But twinkling lights make it less like a junk.
Grandma's got jokes, they make no sense,
Yet we laugh with glee, in this present tense.

Presents that crinkle, oh what could it be?
A sock, a rock, or a new pet bee?
In corners of joy, we find what we crave,
With laughter like bubbles, we joyously wave.

Laughter Sings in Candlelight

Candlelight flickers, shadows do dance,
Uncle Joe's stories, are they true or just chance?
A chicken in reindeer wraps, what a sight,
As we laugh till we cry, oh what pure delight!

Eggnog spills, and glasses are clinked,
A toast for the cookies, well, that's what we think!
Whispers from elves, had too much to say,
And we giggle and chuckle, the night slips away.

Socks on the ceiling, a decoration rare,
Seems like someone was cleaning with flair.
Our hats are too big, but who really cares?
We're all just a family, lost in our flares.

Jingle bells jangle, so loud in the night,
As laughter breaks out, everything feels right.
Wrapped in the glow, we shine like the sun,
In this festive chaos, we have so much fun.

Beneath the Blanket of Snow

Snowflakes surround, like curtains they fall,
Snowman is grinning, but what's that? A stall!
His carrot is missing, oh where can it be?
Perhaps it escaped to take a nice tea!

Sledding down hills with a whoosh and a laugh,
Face full of snow, but we take it in half.
Hot chocolate fights, a drink gone astray,
With marshmallows flying, we call it our play.

Frosty the snowman, he's wobbly and bold,
We give him a hat, in return, we are sold.
But as he melts down, our hearts turn to sigh,
Still laughing with joy, we wave him goodbye.

In winter wonder, we find all the glee,
As snowflakes come down, just wait, you'll see.
Mom's in the kitchen, the cookies a blitz,
While Dad's in the corner, trying on mitts!

Threads Woven from Love

Sweaters are knitted with love and bold flair,
But with arms like a crab, who really could wear?
Grandpa's old tales, they make us all sigh,
While we giggle at memories, oh me, oh my!

Baking disasters, flour everywhere,
An explosion of cupcakes, with frosting to spare.
We dive into sprinkles, like fish in the sea,
In this mess of color, we laugh, can't you see?

Naughty pets ripping the gifts by the tree,
Leaving us wondering, what could it be?
With bows on their tails, they prance like the stars,
While we chase them down, saying, "Oh, what bizarre!"

In stitches and giggles, the fabric unravels,
With love as our thread, on this path, it travels.
Crafted in laughter, with joy so profound,
In these quirky moments, our hearts are unbound.

Echoes of Yuletide Laughter

A jolly old elf, quite chubby and round,
Continues his antics, oh what joy is found!
With a belly that shakes like a bowl full of jelly,
He's always upending a bowl of mashed Smelly!

Rudolph's nose glows, not quite what it seems,
He smashed through the branches of my Christmas dreams.
With a wink and a laugh, he's singing off key,
We're all laughing hard 'til we fall off the tree!

Cookies left out, but where did they go?
Santa's got secrets, as we all know.
I swear those reindeer are plotting a prank,
While munching on treats from my snacky tank!

The cats chase the ribbons, the kids scream with glee,
What's that in my stocking? A rubber ducky!
Each gift brings a giggle, a funny surprise,
Echoes of laughter, oh how the time flies!

Snowflakes' Dance in Twilight

Snowflakes are twirling, caught in the wind,
One landed on my nose, now I'm grinning again!
A snowman's been built, with rocks for a grin,
But he melted too fast—oh where have you been?

Sledding down hills, oh what a wild ride,
I thought I'd be graceful, but I tumbled and cried!
Winter's fierce, swirling, a frosty ballet,
With my scarf on my head, I can't find my way!

Snowball fights happening all over the street,
I duck for cover while dodging the heat!
A fluffy white snowball hit me right in the face,
I laugh it off, but 'twas the cat's great embrace!

Night falls upon us, the stars shine so bright,
The air filled with giggles, oh what a delight.
As snowflakes keep dancing, in giggles we play,
Playing beneath the moonlight, our cares drift away!

Heartbeats Under the Tree

Beneath the great pine, in the glow of the lights,
The dog is dreaming sweetly of Christmas nights.
We hung up the socks, yet they're full of cat toys,
 Heartbeats and laughter; oh what goofy joys!

A tree that's so crooked, it's making me grin,
With ornaments dangling, I might lose a limb!
Kids laughing as they try to climb and peek,
 All eager to see what the season will speak.

Tinsel gets tangled, a feat to behold,
I'm wrapped in the garland, a sight to unfold!
While the cookies are baking, disaster's afoot,
A reindeer shaped cookie just looks like a foot!

Underneath all the laughter, we share silly sighs,
With heartbeats that echo and sparkle like eyes.
The warmth of our moments, so silly yet sweet,
 Together we smirk at the trimmings we meet!

Candles Glimmering in the Night

Candles are glowing, flickering bright,
Casting fun shadows that dance in the night.
A cat on the table, eyeing the pies,
Our feast turns to chaos with jingly surprise!

The lights twinkle softly, while auntie starts singing,
But her voice starts to crack, and the laughter is springing.

With laughter contagious, the room fills with cheer,
The dog steals the ham—it's his perfect career!

Forgotten fond memories, now wrapped up tight,
As giggles erupt in our jolly delight.
So here's to the moments, both silly and bright,
Candles may flicker, but love ignites light!

With games overlapping and mishaps galore,
We gather our hearts, always wanting more.
As the night wraps around us like warmth of a hug,
We toast to the joys, and the love we all tug!

Connections Made in Quiet Moments

In the corner, Grandpa snores,
Dreaming of sugarplums, and more.
A cat in the tree, looking like a star,
Wondering if he's gone too far.

Cookies laid out, the dog takes a bite,
While kids giggle, lighting the night.
Unwrapping laughter, paper goes flying,
Mom rolls her eyes, but she's also trying.

Family chaos, oh what a scene,
Dad wears a sweater that's bright and green.
Tinsel stuck to a reindeer's nose,
The joy of these moments, everyone knows.

A game of charades, so silly and loud,
Uncle pretends he's too big for the crowd.
Yet here in the chaos, the heart finds a way,
To cherish the laughter that brightens the day.

The Gift of Now

Wrap it up tight, that last-minute gift,
Why's it so heavy? It gives me a lift.
Grandma's old fruitcake, now that's a delight,
Should I taste it? I'd rather take flight.

A Christmas tree that looks slightly off,
Ornaments swaying like they're in a scoff.
The kids decorated with sticky fingers,
That's when the real holiday cheer lingers.

Snow falls gently, but wait, what's that?
A snowball surprise, right from the cat!
Laughter erupts in this wintery glow,
Making memories that continue to grow.

So here's to the moments, both silly and bright,
The gift of each giggle in holiday light.
Forget all the worries, just savor the fun,
For in these sweet seconds, we truly have won.

Sealed with Joy and Memories

A letter to Santa, what might it say?
A list full of wishes, he's on his way!
But oh, what's this? It's addressed to me,
Looks like I'm getting that toy on TV!

Tape rolls away, and where's the end?
Wrapping paper battles, we can't quite fend.
It's stuck to my shoe, it's stuck to my hair,
Christmas isn't perfect, but who really cares?

A snowman outside, oh he looks a bit odd,
With a mop for a hat, he's truly a fraud.
Still, we all cheer, "What a sight to behold!"
Magic of moments, more precious than gold.

Looking around, smiles fill the room,
Laughter and joy banishing gloom.
Here's to embracing the mess and the fun,
Sealed with all memories, together as one.

Glistening Paths to Happiness

Sledding down hills, no fear of a crash,
A snowman in uggs? The latest fashion flash!
Parents shake heads, just what can we say?
This is the magic, life's funny display.

Lights on the roof, quite the sight,
Uncle Joe's balance just isn't quite right.
With a flick and a crash, the decorations twirl,
Polar bear pajamas in a wintery whirl!

Carols are sung, slightly off-key,
Creating a symphony of pure holiday glee.
Cookies left out? They disappear fast,
Even the reindeer, they've come here for a blast.

So here's to the laughter, the joy that we chase,
In these glistening paths, we each find a place.
Together we sparkle, like lights on the tree,
In the chaos of love, we're all truly free.

Embracing the Chill with Warmth.

Snowflakes dance like tiny sprites,
Laughter echoes, a pure delight.
Hot cocoa spills, marshmallows fly,
Mom's new reindeer socks make us sigh.

Frosty noses, cheeks so red,
Uncle Fred in a Santa bed.
We trip on tinsel, laugh on cue,
Oh, Christmas chaos, we love you!

Gifts all wrapped with sticky tape,
A cat in a box? What a shape!
Picking pine needles from the floor,
Who knew this time could be such a chore?

Yet in the mess, joy's in the air,
Giggles escaping everywhere.
We embrace the chill, hearts so bright,
In our cozy house, it feels just right.

Silent Whispers of Frost

The snow falls silent, shh, not a peep,
While we chase snowmen, piled up deep.
Whispers of frost, secrets in the night,
As snowballs fly with all our might.

In pajamas, we build a grand fort,
The pillow fight? Best kind of sport!
Grandma's cookies, a scrumptious treat,
Baking disasters? Oh, what a feat!

The dog runs by, his tongue all fluffed,
A pair of warm socks? Now that's stuffed!
We giggle at the scenes we create,
'Til we trip on the rug, oh, what a fate!

But through the laughter and clumsy cheer,
Warm hearts embrace the magic here.
For in every stumble, every grin,
The spirit of joy, we bask in.

Joy Beneath the Mistletoe

Beneath the mistletoe, we stand,
A goofy grin, a clumsy hand.
A peck on the cheek? Not quite the plan,
But giggles erupt, oh, what a man!

Uncle Joe's jokes, all in bad taste,
Cringeworthy puns, but never a waste.
It's the laughter that lights up the room,
Winter's chill vanished, gone like our gloom!

The cat swipes at garlands with flair,
As Auntie serves soup, we all share the scare.
Grandpa's shrug at our silly displays,
Their eyes all twinkle in a playful haze.

Yet underneath all this festive fuss,
Love's the thread that binds us, we trust.
So here's to the fun, both sweet and absurd,
In joyful moments, our hearts have stirred.

Starlit Halls of Merriment

In starlit halls where giggles rise,
We dance like elves, oh what a surprise!
A twirl here, a trip there, oh dear me,
Spinning around with zest, so carefree!

The punch bowl tips; a splashy delight,
A mix of flavors that's quite a sight.
Friends all around, wearing foam hats,
We're decking the halls with silly spats!

Three-legged races and caroling tunes,
Singing out loud, out of sync like loons.
Frosty windows, with sugar on top,
As we toast with our juice, we'll never stop!

Here's to the joy that glows so bright,
In starlit halls, our hearts take flight.
We embrace the silly, let laughter renew,
For in these moments, life feels brand new.

Envelopes of Cheer and Connection

In the mailbox, a card appears,
With glitter, sparkles, and maybe some tears.
Uncle Joe's face, with a reindeer hat,
Makes me wonder, is he really that fat?

The tree's adorned, with tinsel and glee,
But the cat thinks it's a jungle spree.
Baubles rolling, a chase all around,
My phone's out of battery, oh, joy, what a sound!

Cookies in plenty, they slowly do vanish,
But auntie's fruitcake? Oh, how to banish!
I'll feed it to Fido, who just gives a stare,
What recipe calls for this much despair?

Presents wrapped tight, with tape all in knots,
No fingerprints left, it's a mess that it spots.
But laughter and love are the best kinds of glue,
In these silly times, I'm just happy with you!

Seasons Change but Love Remains

Snowflakes fall, but socks disappear,
Each year they vanish, yet none shed a tear.
Mom's making soup, with a dash of pure love,
But dad's in the fridge, snacking like a dove.

Carols blasting—oh, what a delight!
But the dog starts howling, trying to join the fight.
Grandma's out dancing on the living room floor,
She spins like a top, we can't take it anymore!

The lights twinkle bright, but one's gone astray,
Uncle Phil insists it'll come back someday.
Meanwhile, Aunt Sue's tangled in the cords,
Her expression says everything, in many words!

Cookies and laughter, like a big warm hug,
Every sweet moment, snug as a bug.
So here's to the chaos, the jingle bell cheer,
In this joyful season, I'm glad you are here!

Frost-kissed Laughter

Snowflakes tumble, kids in flight,
Hot cocoa spills, what a sight!
Sleds go whizzing, laughter loud,
A snowman's nose, a carrot proud.

Tickle fights with mittens on,
Snowball splats, you can't be wrong!
Winter's chill, yet faces glow,
Jingle bells, oh what a show!

Candy canes all stuck in hair,
Grandpa's dance, a funny flare!
Pine needles on the living room floor,
Socks thrown high, then in a roar!

Gifts that rattle, secrets squeal,
Unwrap the fun, oh what a deal!
Frosty breath, a giggle spree,
This season's magic, wild and free.

The Spirit that Unites Us

Monkeys in pajamas, what a craze,
Grandma's cookies, a chocolate maze!
A Christmas sweater, bright and bold,
Worn with pride despite the cold.

Elf hats wobble on tiny heads,
Singing songs while jumping on beds!
Mismatched socks and joy combined,
Unified laughter, oh how it shines!

Popping popcorn, strands to string,
Lights that flicker, oh how they sing!
Uncle Joe tries to mime a deer,
Silly moments, all gathered near.

Chasing pets with reindeer horns,
Holiday quirks, we laugh till worn!
Joyful noise, an echo bright,
In every heart, there's pure delight.

Echoes of Old Favorites

Carols ringing, out of tune,
Sing along beneath the moon!
That old vinyl, scratchy cheer,
Reminds us of days, warm and dear.

Unwrapped memories, wrapped so tight,
Old sweaters bring a big delight!
Familiar tales of Santa's flight,
Lost in laughter, we take flight!

Popcorn kernels pop and dance,
In the kitchen, chaos, chance!
Jokes and laughter we can share,
In every gift, love fills the air.

Grandma's stories, each a tease,
"I swear I saw you climb those trees!"
Friends and family, all unite,
In echoes sweet, this joyous night.

Radiance in a Child's Eyes

Tiny hands reach up so high,
A twinkling tree lights up the sky!
Giggles echo, pure delight,
As dreams take flight on frosty nights.

Bright-eyed wonder, oh what glee,
To share this joy, just you and me!
Ribbons flying in a rush,
Wrapping paper, hear that hush!

Joyful whispers spark the air,
Wishing stars, we're free from care!
Each moment cherished, held so tight,
In every gaze, there's purest light.

Spinning 'round, in snowflakes deep,
The laughter and the joy we keep!
One more cookie? Oh yes, please!
In hearts, we find our blissful keys.